What Adults Don't Know About Architecture

Published in 2020 by The School of Life
First published in the USA in 2021
70 Marchmont Street, London WC1N 1AB

Copyright © The School of Life 2020
Design and illustrations by Studio Katie Kerr

Printed in Latvia by Livonia

The School of Life offers programmes, publications and
services to assist modern individuals in their quest to live
more engaged and meaningful lives. We've also developed
a collection of content-rich, design-led retail products to
promote useful insights and ideas from culture.

www.theschooloflife.com

ISBN 978-1-912891-30-6

10 9 8 7 6 5 4 3 2

What Adults Don't Know About Architecture

Inspiring young minds to build
a more beautiful world

THE SCHOOL OF LIFE PRESS

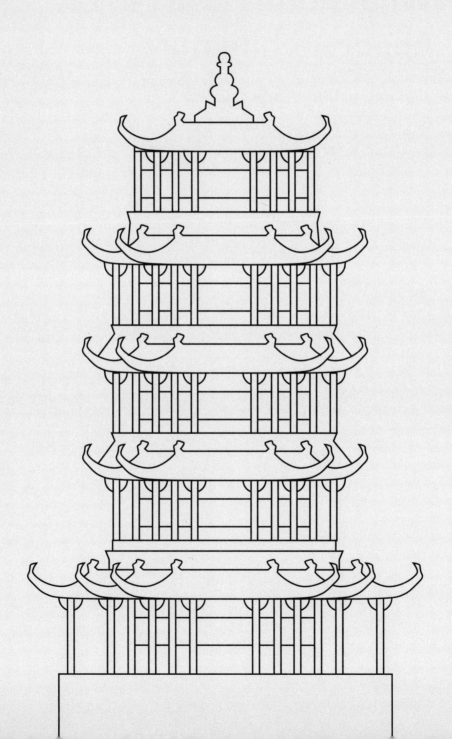

Contents

An Introduction to Architecture

You're an architect!   1
Why is architecture important?   9
How buildings are like people   11
Why are so many places ugly?   24
What is beauty?   27
The recipe for good architecture   57

How to Build a Beautiful City

Make your city interesting   67
Become a team manager   77
Make things the right size   88
Use nice materials   106
Develop a local style   120
Make the city lively   140
Repetition is good   156

Conclusion

Why are houses so expensive?   171
Architecture and democracy   178

An Introduction to Architecture

You're an architect!

Architecture is the business of designing buildings: houses, streets, towns and cities. If someone asked you, "Are you interested in architecture?" you might feel unsure what to say. But, probably without realising it, you've been interested in architecture for a long time. Maybe one day at the beach you built a great sandcastle with towers at each corner.

A sandcastle on Morro Strand State Beach, California, USA

Or perhaps when you were little you made a cottage using red and black bricks. Or maybe you did a drawing once of your dream house, with a pool and a slide instead of stairs.

Maybe one day you tried living in a blanket fort for the afternoon (it was a good idea until you tried to stand up), or perhaps you dreamed about the perfect tree house:

The perfect tree house, Quebec, Canada

Without quite knowing it, you have designed buildings: you're an architect!

You already understand the most important thing about architecture: You know the kinds of buildings you like and the kinds of buildings you don't like.

Perhaps one time in the countryside you saw an interesting house like this one. It seemed like a lovely place to live. It would be fun to sleep under the thatched roof, and nice to come home in winter knowing how cosy it would be inside.

Selworthy, Somerset, UK, early 19th century

But thinking about living in this house made you feel a bit sad:

A suburban house in Belgium, 19th/20th century

Or you went on holiday to Greece and saw a street like this:

Mykonos, Greece

It's the little street you walked down to get from the hotel
to the beach. Although it was very sunny, the street was nice
and shady. There was a tiny shop around the corner where

they sold ice cream. In the evenings the people who lived on the street would sit out on their balconies or walk up and down chatting to their neighbours.

Then imagine that at another time you had to come here:

Athens, Greece

It was crowded and noisy, and even a bit scary. It wouldn't be a nice place to walk around in the evening.

And perhaps once your mum or dad showed you an old photograph of where they lived in Europe before you were born. They were living in a top-floor flat on a street like this:

Vienna, Austria

It was quite busy but there were lots of trees and interesting shops and they said it was fun living in the centre of the city near all their friends. They could walk everywhere in a few minutes. All the buildings are packed together, but if you look at them carefully each building is quite beautiful.

But then they showed you another picture from a time when they were away on a work trip:

New York, USA

They said there were hardly any attractive buildings (and none at all near their hotel), and there was no point even trying to cross the road, as it would take so long. You couldn't really walk anywhere, in fact. You had to take a taxi and then it would get stuck in traffic.

In other words, you realise that some places are much nicer than others.

And sadly, most buildings are not very nice and only a few buildings and places are really lovely. That's deeply unfair and unnecessary.

In this book we're going to talk about what makes some places lovely. We're not just doing so for the sake of it:

We want to understand how to get more good architecture into the world.

Kyoto, Japan

But we don't only want to understand. Understanding how to make nice buildings and places is the first step to actually making more nice places. That's the real goal. We can't do it on our own. We're going to need your help! Together we will build a more beautiful world.

Why is architecture important?

Does it matter what a place looks like? If most people have somewhere to live and work, and they can get about and there are shops and hospitals and schools, isn't that enough?

We think that what a place looks like matters a lot.

One of the reasons why what places look like matters a lot is that buildings speak to us about things. Not actually by talking, but metaphorically — by sending us messages.

When buildings are beautiful, it is as though they are speaking about lovely things, like kindness, hope and trust. And when they are ugly, it is as though they are speaking about hatred, aggression and nastiness. Imagine a place you were in was speaking to you. What might it be saying?

Your favourite street in Greece might say something like this:

I am very gentle, playful and sweet. I care about you. That's why I want you to have a lovely balcony where you can sit and have a really interesting conversation. I want you to be able to stroll down the street without having to worry that a car is going to bump into you.

I have got soft sides. I believe in friendship. I like it that anyone can wave to you from their window. I think calm is important. That's why I wear soothing colours: I don't want you to feel agitated. I hope you'll be happy here.

Whereas the place your Mum went on a work trip might say something like this:

I care more about cars than about you; I care a lot about advertising, so I am going to make you look at a huge sign every single day of your life, even if you never want to buy the product it is selling. I am often in a bad mood. Your little sorrows and pains don't matter to me. Life is tough and I don't care. I don't know who you are and I don't ever want to know.

You may not be consciously aware that streets are beaming messages at you all the time. But the messages sink deep into your brain nevertheless.

Like a person, a building or a place can be friendly or hostile, kindly or uncaring, generous or mean. If you spend time in these places it eventually has a big impact on your sense of who you are. An interesting person* once put it like this:

We shape our buildings and afterwards our buildings shape us.

* The 20th-century British Prime Minister, Winston Churchill.

How buildings are like people

It is not just streets that speak to us — every building has a personality. Let's meet some different types of building and think about what they might be like.

What kind of personality do you think this old building has?

Sackville House, East Grinstead, England, c. 1520

It's gentle and cosy, a bit like an old teddy bear. It's not very adventurous, but it's lovely when you're feeling tired or a bit sad. It listens quietly to your troubles and it is always there — reassuring and comfortable.

Or what about this building?

Green Chemical Futures, Clayton, Australia, 2015

This one feels like it's always rushing about, trying to grab your attention and tell you something about itself (even if you're not in the mood); it's like it is always saying:

Everyone, look at me! Look at me!

This little house in Japan is very calm. If you have had a busy, tricky day at school it would be nice to sit on the veranda with the garden all around you. Even if it was raining it wouldn't matter because the wide roof would protect you.

Uchihashi-tei tea house, Kenrokuen Gardens, Kanazawa, Japan, 1774

It's soothing; it's not going to ask you lots of questions about what happened in your maths lesson or where you left your sports shoes. Instead it might say:

Come in, sit down. Let's have a cup of tea.

Whereas, this skyscraper looks like it would just ignore you: It doesn't say hello, ask you how you are or how your day was.

Marriott Hotel, The Centrum LIM skyscraper, Warsaw, Poland, 1989

If you say something to this building it would pretend it has not heard you, and if you ever did manage to have a conversation, it would probably be very boring.

This is a rather smart building — it is very well organised, determined and polite.

If you were going on a trip, this building would get to the airport in plenty of time; it would never forget anyone's passport. It doesn't need to be fussy or anxious because it's already got everything under control. It might say:

Come on, let's get our homework done,
so it's out of the way.

The next house is the Villa Savoye (named after the Savoye family who first lived there). It was built in around 1930 by a French-Swiss architect called Charles-Édouard Jeanneret, but he's better known by the nickname 'Le Corbusier'.

It looks a bit like a spaceship that's hovering just above Earth, ready to land, or maybe to take off on a fantastic adventure. This house likes experimenting and trying out new things:

Villa Savoye, Poissy, France, 1931

This house isn't nice but it wants you to think it's fantastic:

An example of a 'McMansion', Missouri, USA, 20th century

It goes around boasting to everyone, even though it has not really got much to boast about. It's keen to tell you it has lots of cars because (secretly) it feels you probably don't like it.

This Scottish castle is telling us something quite different:

Eilean Donan Castle, Scotland, 13th century

It was built hundreds of years ago, and it's brave and strong, but not at all frightening — in fact, it is the opposite of a bully because it uses its strength to make you feel safe. If someone was bothering you it would always stand up for you.

You might guess the name of the next one: the Glass House!

Glass House, Connecticut, USA, 1948–1949

The Glass House was designed in 1948 by an American architect called Philip Johnson, as his own house. It's made of glass on all sides, so you can look out and see the grass and the big trees from every direction. He had to build a round wall in the middle though — to hide the bathroom.

This house likes to try to get things clear — if something was worrying you it would help you get to the root of the problem, and figure out what you could do about it. It's not stern or nosey: It's on your side. It just knows that if you don't panic and you take your time and think carefully, you'll be able to find good answers to most upsetting or annoying issues.

Every individual part of a building has a personality too. Imagine this window was a person, what kind of person might it be?

George Eastman Museum, New York, USA, 1905

The ivy-framed window is friendly, but maybe a little bit shy: the middle part edges forward, but not much. It is as if the window wants to say hello but it's not feeling very confident at the moment. It's rather sweet but also modest.

This is a very different kind of window. It was made in the 18th century in Russia:

It has quite an exciting personality — rather talkative and full of ideas. It doesn't like being quiet and could easily get bored and restless. This window doesn't want to sit still or spend a cosy evening inside in front of the television; it wants to go to a party, dance the night away and have fun.

A famous philosopher called Ludwig Wittgenstein helped design this house in Vienna in the 1920s for his older sister, Margaret Stonborough-Wittgenstein.

Haus Wittgenstein, Vienna, Austria, 1928

Wittgenstein spent a long time getting the windows just right. Like him, they are serious and thoughtful. These windows don't like making a fuss — they want to get on and get things done, and they are not interested in chit-chat or small talk. They are very honest and straightforward.

This is part of a famous house in Scotland called the Hill House (because it's on a hill). It was designed in around 1900 by someone called Charles Rennie Mackintosh. He wanted the house to look modern, but he wanted it to be cosy inside as well. The owner was a man called Walter Blackie, who published books for children.

Hill House, Helensbugh, Scotland, 1902–1904

This window doesn't mind being on its own; in fact, that is sometimes what it likes most — though it can get lonely too. It likes looking at the hills or imagining what it would be like to be a bird or to be in a ship sailing on a distant ocean.

Every time you see a building you can ask a very helpful set of questions. The first question is:

What kind of person is this building?

The second question is:

If this building were speaking to me,
what would it be speaking about?

Being around buildings is like being around people. It makes a big difference if you are surrounded by kind, interesting people or surrounded by boring, unfriendly people. Nice people can help you to develop the best parts of yourself: in their company you can grow and develop well. But imagine you mostly spent time with mean people: it would be hard to be yourself, and you would always be anxious, wary and worried.

As we have discovered, buildings and places can be friendly or unfriendly and kindly or mean. And that's why it matters such a lot what kinds of places we build.

Imagine a world in which more buildings speak to us about the nicest things.

Why are so many places ugly?

A lot of buildings and places are rather ugly. They are like unkind people, and they're sending unfriendly messages to us. So *why* are there so many of them?

If you ask an adult why there are so many places in the world that are ugly, they might say:

Because it costs too much to make nice places.

It sounds like a sensible answer. Quite often, good things do cost a lot. Not everyone can have a really great car because great cars cost so much money. Luxury hotels are very nice, but not everyone can stay in them because the prices are so high. So maybe it is the same with architecture. Maybe it just is that lovely buildings cost too much, so we can't afford to have very many of them.

But with architecture this is not really a very good answer. Actually, some of the most attractive buildings were made by people who didn't have much money at all. The blue and white street in the Greek Islands we were looking at on page 4 was originally built for quite poor people to live in. It was cheap housing, but it was also really nice.

You can see it this way, too: Imagine you give two people the same number of plastic bricks and ask them to make a house:

One person might make something brilliant and the other person might make something horrible. The difference is not to do with how many bricks they used but with how nice their ideas were. Nicer ideas don't cost more money.

Or an adult might say:

The lovely places are lovely because they are old. The ugly places are ugly because they are new. There's nothing we can do about that except wait. Maybe in 2235 people will think that our busy road lined with tower blocks and our shopping centres are beautiful and they'll make special trips just to visit them.

But this isn't a good answer either. It says that a new building or street or city just can't be beautiful until many years have passed — and that doesn't make sense. That would be like saying it's impossible to make a beautiful pair of shoes or a nice car or write a beautiful song these days — but obviously we can do these things. Why should it only be nice buildings that we can't make now? And anyway, as we'll see, there are plenty of really wonderful modern streets and buildings.

We think the answer is very different. We think there are so many ugly places in the world because of mistaken ideas. The difference between nice places and ugly places is not to do with how much they cost or when they were built. The difference between 'nice' and 'ugly' is to do with how people *think* about architecture.

That's what this book is all about. Together we are going to be looking for good ideas about how to build well. We want to understand which ideas lead to amazing buildings and beautiful places. Each of the chapters in this book explores one big, important — and good — idea for architecture. We will get to all the good ideas quite soon, but first we're going to look at one very big mistake that leads to ugly streets and cities. It's this:

We think we can't say what beauty is.

Maybe it's not obvious why this is *such a disaster*.
So we're going to take a bit of time to see why it is...

What is beauty?

Nowadays it seems pretty strange to ask questions about beauty. If you ask a grown-up, or an architect, what makes a building or a city beautiful they would probably squirm a bit, look embarrassed and say that they don't really know. Or they might just say that everyone has their own ideas about beauty and we can't possibly say which is best or right. So perhaps we had better not talk about beauty at all.

Paro Taktsang 'Tiger's Nest', Paro Valley, Bhutan, 17th century

This feels like the obvious response to a lot of people today, but actually for most of human history (and in lots of different places) people all agreed about what made a building beautiful. For example, for most of the history of Europe and North America, people thought that if you wanted to make a beautiful building or a beautiful street or a beautiful city, all you had to do was follow the rules of classical architecture. But what did people mean by this?

Beginning in Italy in around 1400, people started looking around and asking themselves which buildings they most liked in the whole world. They decided it wasn't any of the recent buildings. Instead, they much preferred the very old buildings and ruins that had survived from classical antiquity — that is, from the time when ancient Rome ruled a lot of the world. They then made new buildings that were pretty similar to the really old ones. They called this 'classical' architecture, because it involved learning lessons from 'classical' antiquity.

Here are some of the things built by the ancient Romans that these people particularly admired and some new buildings made based on them.

The first temple was completed in the 2nd century CE in Nîmes in the South of France. It was admired for its very logical design and for its strong, unbroken lines. The Romans built lots of temples, all pretty much like this.

Maison Carrée, Nîmes, France, c. 2nd century CE

The church below was built in Paris in the 1840s. It's almost an exact copy of the temple — only a lot bigger.

La Madeleine, Paris, France, 1842

The ruins below are part of an enormous palace that was built for the Roman Emperor Hadrian in the countryside outside of Rome in the 2nd century CE. What people liked was the way the row of columns curves gently round the pond.

It feels a bit like they're going to give you a hug.

These colonnades (a row of columns supporting a roof) were built in St Peter's Square in Rome in the 1600s by an architect called Gian Lorenzo Bernini:

St Peter's Square, Rome, Italy, 1656–1667

If you look closely you can see they are modelled on the curving row of columns at Hadrian's palace.

Another example from the 2nd century CE is this very old building in Rome in Italy called the Pantheon. *Pan* means 'all' in Ancient Greek, which, confusingly, was the language educated Romans liked to use.

Pantheon, Rome, Italy, 2nd century CE

It was originally built as a circular domed temple to the Roman gods, but since the 7th century the Pantheon has been used as a Catholic church dedicated to 'St Mary and the Martyrs'.

The picture below is the most important building at the University of Virginia in the United States. It is called the Rotunda which means a round building or room. Another example of a rotunda is St Paul's Cathedral on page 99.

The Rotunda, University of Virginia, Virginia, USA, 1822–1826

It was designed in the 1820s by Thomas Jefferson, who had been the American president from 1801 to 1809. Jefferson wanted it to look just like the Pantheon.

In Jefferson's case though, the building housed books rather than being a temple, which was unusual because at that time in other universities in the English-speaking world books were typically kept in churches.

In the 4th century CE this arch was constructed in the middle of Rome to celebrate victory in an important battle.

Arch of Constantine, Rome, Italy, c. 315 CE

Later on, people admired the sense of balance and harmony in the monument. They particularly liked the way that the very top of the side arches just come up to the 'springing line'* of the arch in the middle.

The enormous house on the next page was built in England in the 1760s. The central part above the curving staircases was closely based on the Arch of Constantine in Rome.

* That's the point where it starts to curve.

Kedleston Hall, Derbyshire, England, 1765

Classical architecture followed a *recipe*, just like one you'd find in a cookbook.

Take, for example a recipe for pizza Margherita, which may be the most popular kind of pizza in the world. The topping is made up of tomatoes, mozzarella cheese and basil leaves.

A pizza like this was made in 1889 for the King and Queen of Italy. The queen's name was Margherita and the chef who made it very politely named it in her honour. That could have been the end of the story — there might have only ever been one pizza using exactly these ingredients — but someone wrote down the recipe. That meant that anyone could copy it. If you follow the recipe you can make pretty much the same pizza at home as often as you want.

Classical architecture used recipes in the same way. There were lots of 'building recipe books' that gave people all the rules they needed to follow when they were making a door or a window, and the 'recipes' showed them how to use columns and arches correctly.

These books told architects how to make the roof and what height a building should be — they went into a lot of detail. There were lots of different books all explaining the same kinds of recipes in slightly different ways.

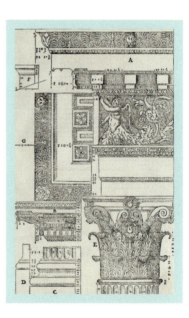

Andrea Palladio, The Four Books of Architecture, 1570

These are pages from a book by the most famous maker of architectural recipes, called Andrea Palladio. He only built a few buildings himself, and they're all in Italy. But people everywhere read his book.

Using these recipe books, architects built many, many thousands of buildings in the classical style. In fact, in large parts of the world, for hundreds of years, practically every important building was built following the classical rules.

People could build lots and lots of buildings that would all match up.

Like this square, for example. In the middle of the 18th century the centre of the French town of Nancy was built using a classical recipe book.

In the early 18th century, Peter the Great, the Tsar of Russia, built a huge new capital city, called St Petersburg.*

General Staff Building, St Petersburg, Russia, 1819–1829

The city was designed using a recipe so that the whole city looked like it was in the same style.

Between 1767 and 1890, a large, new part of the Scottish city of Edinburgh (called the New Town) was developed in the classical style. There are hundreds of streets and squares all following the same recipes.

* He very modestly named it after himself.

So, for a very long time in history, in much of the world, there was actually a lot of agreement about what makes a building, and therefore a city, beautiful. They thought:

You just have to follow the classical recipes
and you'll be sure to make something nice.

Then everything started to change. One thing that happened was travel. Around 1850 the world started to become covered with railway lines. Steam ships were invented that were much faster and more reliable than the old sailing ships. It became much easier to visit other countries.

People went to China and they saw things like this:

The Temple of Heaven, Beijing, China, 1406–1420

This building has a beautiful name: the Temple of Heaven.

It's a wonderful building, but it's not at all classical. Classical architects would have been very bothered by the way the wide roofs stick out above the round walls.

Then people went to India and they saw buildings like this, the Taj Mahal:

Taj Mahal, Agra, India, 1631–1648

They thought it was lovely, but it didn't follow the classical recipe books — the rules said that domes should never get wider as they go up.

Another thing that happened was that people became more interested in history. They got excited by the things that were built after the Romans but before the classical rules got going again. Conveniently, they called this period the 'Middle Ages'.

What impressed them most from this period of time were the Cathedrals. They especially liked this one, which is in a city in the South of England called Canterbury.

Canterbury Cathedral, Kent, England, 597 (rebuilt 1070–1077)

Many people thought Canterbury Cathedral was a fantastic building, but it broke lots of rules of classical architecture. It wasn't symmetrical and the windows had pointed arches at the top, rather than smooth, round ones.

They quite liked castles, too. Classical architects would say the roofs on this *chateau* (French for castle) in France are too pointy — and you need a lot more windows, and they are not in the right places anyway! But actually, people realised it was very nice.

Château de Vitré, Ille-et-Vilaine, France, 11th century (rebuilt 13th century)

So, now there was a problem! Lots of people had very different ideas about what made a building beautiful. And people had furious arguments — they asked questions like:

Are pointed windows better than rounded windows?
Do buildings have to be symmetrical?
Does it matter if you use columns or not?

Some people got very confused. In this building from the 1890s they have tried to cram lots of different ideas together: a classical window, a very unclassical turret above it and the roof of a farmhouse. Because they couldn't decide, the result was a bit of a mess:

On the next page is another example, the Morey Mansion, where there is a battle going on: one of the roofs (in the middle) slopes up and comes from a French recipe, another roof (on the left) is from a Russian recipe and the windows follow a classical recipe (but overall it is not at all classical, with lots of bits sticking out at odd angles, which classical architects would have hated).

Morey Mansion, California, USA, 1890

Eventually people stopped arguing. They gave up, and started to think that there was no right answer and that no building was better than any other, in terms of how it looks. You can discuss whether a building is strong, if it costs too much to build, if it is easy to heat or cool or if it's got enough rooms, but you can't discuss whether it is beautiful or not.

Everyone came to think that in the end, each person has his or her own ideas about beauty and there's no point in talking about it. In a way it sounds like a very kindly idea:

Let's not have these arguments any more. Let's just let everyone like whatever they happen to like and not try to say what is beautiful or is not.

It even started to feel rather rude to express a strong opinion about beauty. This is the 'anything goes' attitude, because it suggests that it does not matter what a building looks like. But this attitude turned out to be a disaster...

St George Wharf, London, England, 2007–2010

Cumbernauld town centre, Scotland, 1963–1967

46

High rise flats, Hillfields, Coventry, England, c.1960s

One consequence was that lots and lots of buildings that no one really liked were built.

An astonishing number of places ended up looking chaotic, muddled and unfriendly.

At the moment when people talk about architecture they say 'anything goes'. They don't want to say that some places are beautiful and some places are ugly.

But when you look at what people *do* then the story is very different. You can see this with tourism. Tourism tells us about where people like to go just to have a nice time.

Let's look at one of the most popular cities in all of the world. It's visited by 30 million tourists every year — Venice, in Italy.

You might think there isn't anything exciting to do there — there are no theme parks and hardly any shops. And yet millions of people go there just for one thing: to look at the buildings and walk around the beautiful streets and squares.

Grand Canal, Basilica Santa Maria, Venice, Italy

Starting about a thousand years ago, the city of Venice was slowly built on a group of little islands. So instead of roads and streets, there are lots of canals and hundreds of small bridges. There are no cars at all.

By about 1500, Venice was the most important city in the world. The main thing people spent time on was architecture, because they wanted their city to be the most beautiful in the world — and maybe they succeeded. Since about 1800 there hasn't been much new building, so it still looks pretty much the same as it did 200 years ago.

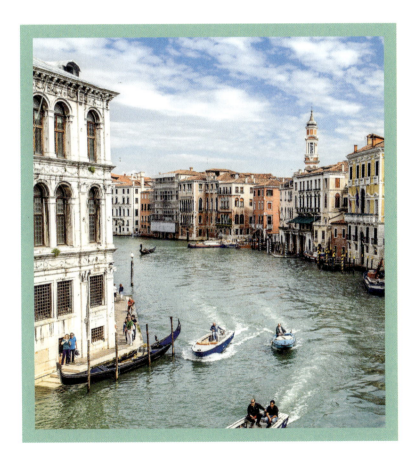

Canal Grande, Venice, Italy

Venice is one of the most visited cities in the world for one main reason: It is so beautiful.

If we list the places that people visit just to look at, they are all very beautiful. Take Kyoto, in Japan. It gets about 50 million visitors a year. People go to Kyoto because it's so lovely:

Kinkaku-ji temple, Kyoto, Japan, 1397

Paris gets 30 million visitors a year, and one of the reasons they go there is because the buildings are so nice to look at:

Observatory of the Sorbonne, Paris, France, 1885-1901

Now let's look at some places that don't get visited by tourists very much at all. Pretty much nobody wants to travel to these cities just to walk round and enjoy the view.

The reason no one visits these places is fairly obvious: They're not that interesting to look at. If you live there you have to put up with it — no one would make a trip just to see them.

By looking at places that tourists choose to visit (and don't) we can see that in terms of what we actually *do*, there is generally agreement about what is a beautiful place and what is an ugly place. We say we don't know what beauty is, but we reliably head off to the beautiful places and avoid the ugly ones if we can.

The terrible thing is that because there's only a few beautiful places — and lots of ugly ones — the lovely places often get very overcrowded with visitors or they become impossibly expensive because everyone wants to live there.

Rue Crémieux, Paris, France

This colourful row of houses has become one of the most photographed streets in Paris. It's lovely, but it now gets so many visitors that the people who live there can't enjoy it.

The street used to be quiet and calm; now it's always crowded with people taking photos of their front doors or looking in their windows to see what the houses are like inside.

In London, these houses have all been divided up into small flats but they are still extremely expensive — because they're so beautiful, and therefore in high demand.

Charlotte Street, Primrose Hill, London, England

The same thing happened to the city of Venice: It's become overcrowded with visitors every day of the year. The people who actually live there have a terrible time. Even if they just want to go to the shops they have to fight their way through crowds of tourists.

Piazza San Marco (St Mark's Square), Venice, Italy

We're in trouble because we have stopped making very beautiful buildings and places.

Our mistaken idea that 'anything goes' in architecture has caused us to build a lot of places that don't actually look very nice. And because we have stopped making beautiful places, there aren't very many of them around. So the ones that do exist become so crowded and expensive that we can't easily enjoy them.

Imagine that for some reason only about 100 smartphones had ever been made. They would still be amazing, but hardly anyone would get to use one. And they would be extraordinarily expensive — each one would probably sell for millions of pounds. If you were allowed to try one out for free the queue would stretch for miles and miles.

Of course, this has not happened with phones for a very obvious reason: Instead of just making 100 good phones, about 8 billion of them have been produced.

What happened was that people worked out the *recipe* for making top-quality mobile phones. It was hard to work out the recipe, but once it had been discovered it was pretty easy to make more and more phones. So now nearly everyone on the planet has a mobile phone that works well and looks nice (and can take cool photos of architecture!).

La Trobe Reading Room, Melbourne, Australia, 1913

We would like this to happen with architecture. We think it's terrible that only a few cities are truly beautiful, so we want to do again for architecture the same thing that happened for phones (and for Margherita pizzas!). We need a new recipe for making beautiful places so that one day everyone can live somewhere really nice.

The recipe for good architecture

Making a recipe for good architecture depends on one key thing:

Explaining *why* you like what you like.

Why is this canal in Venice so lovely?

This idea will be used a lot in the rest of the book, so let's see if we can get the hang of it now.

Take a look at the two streets below. Which one do you prefer? Which one looks nicer or more beautiful?

Accordia housing development, Cambridge, England, 2003–2011

Gilpin Place, Cambridge, England

We're guessing that you prefer the one at the top, but can you explain *why* you like that street more than the other one?

If you want to make a recipe, it is not enough just to decide which you prefer. You have to try to work out the reasons why one is nicer than the other.

You have to go from a *feeling* to an *explanation*.

Providing reasons or explanations for your feelings is the same as working out the ingredients and instructions for a recipe. Just liking a particular kind of pizza is fine, but that feeling won't help you to make that kind of pizza yourself. To make the pizza, you need to know the ingredients and how to use them: You need to find an *explanation* for what makes that pizza nice.

To help us understand this better, let's do an experiment. Try to write down the reasons why you think more people might like the street on the top rather than the one on the bottom. See if you can come up with five reasons for each. It can be quite difficult putting the reasons into words!

When you've had a go at the experiment, turn the page and see how your answers compare with our suggestions. Don't worry if your answers aren't the same as ours.

THE FIRST STREET

There are lots of trees
and plants everywhere

It has a nice path with
stones, and the path is
not exactly in the middle

The top of the houses
are back from the path,
so that the space gets
wider as you look up

There are big windows,
some of them with nice
wooden surrounds, but
they're not too obvious

The brick pillars are all
in a neat row with nice
openings at the top of
the chimneys

THE SECOND STREET

There are hardly any
plants and no trees

The grey road goes
right up to the houses,
so there's no garden

Odd bits of the buildings
jut out weirdly, and the
buildings are different
on each side

There are lots of blank
walls and the window
on the right looks a bit
squashed against the
railing in front of it

There is a car parked in
the street, which makes
it seem less nice

Working out the reasons why you like a place is useful
because it gives you the recipe for making more places
that are nice in the same kind of way.

Let's try it out. Imagine you are walking around the nice street we've just been looking at. You look at the buildings from different angles and walk up and down the path...

A different view of the Accordia housing development

And while you're walking, all the time you're asking yourself:

What did they do here that makes this place nice? What's the recipe?

On the next page, we've put together a recipe for this street.

Recipe for a housing development

STEP ONE

Make sure you use a really attractive material.
In this case, pale bricks that have a soft texture,
so it's nice to run your hand gently across them.

STEP TWO

Make sure the distance between the buildings is just
a little more than their height. This is about *proportion*:
how high versus how far apart. The idea of proportion
in architecture is similar to proportion in cooking: so
just like you might need three times as much flour as
sugar to make a cake, you need a certain amount of
space for a certain amount of houses when building.
It feels nice in this street because the buildings feel
cosy (not too tall), but they're not so close together
that it feels claustrophobic. By recognising this, you
are understanding the reason (the part of the recipe)
that gives you this nice feeling.

STEP THREE

Push the upper floors of the buildings back a little.
This means you get a nice balcony space up there
and you can look down on the path and gardens.
It also means that you do not feel squashed or
restricted as you walk along the path.

STEP FOUR

Use lots of plants, but think carefully about their colours. Here it's mostly green, which looks pretty against the pale brick, but they've also used a bit of greyish-purple for the stones under the trees.

STEP FIVE

Make a pergola (the wooden thing in the middle), so one day more plants will grow up around it. Let the unpainted wood fade to a gentle grey colour.

STEP SIX

Build high chimneys. This sounds odd, because you might not imagine that it would look good, but here it does. Why is that? The chimneys are tall and slender, they're nicely spaced out and they have little holes at the top, so it looks as if they've got tiny battlements.

STEP SEVEN

This is a curious one. In the pictures you can't see the windows of the houses. They have big windows but it's not so obvious. Why might that be nice? If you live here you'd like to look at the garden, but you do not want people staring in all the time. So the plants and chimneys help keep the windows slightly out of view.

Hide the cars and garages. One of the nicest things about this street is that the cars use a back lane, so there aren't cars in front of the houses or unattractive garages spoiling the view. It is funny — maybe the cleverest idea here is something you don't see!

The steps in this recipe are all closely connected to the reasons why this place is nice. The reasons give you the recipe! And now, if you wanted, you could go off and build your own version of a street a bit like this and it would be lovely too.

Some people worry that they can't be architects because they can't think of brand new ideas for buildings. But actually that doesn't matter, because:

The way you design beautiful places is by reusing the best recipes that already exist.

How to Build
a Beautiful City

We want you to build a beautiful city — not a pretend one, a real one!

Maybe that sounds ridiculous? You're too young, you haven't been trained as an architect and building cities costs huge amounts of money.

But perhaps one day you really could do it — because what's most important for building beautiful cities are *ideas* and *recipes*. Good ideas and good recipes make good cities.

Money isn't really the problem, because enormous amounts of money are being spent on making new buildings every single day all round the world without good results.

The hard part isn't getting things built:

The hard (and most important) part is understanding what is best to build.

In the next part of the book we're going to figure out the different steps needed to create the recipe for nicer cities. We'll look at what's gone well and what's gone badly up to now to help us discover which ideas work and which ideas are a bit of a disaster. We have not got all the right ideas, but we think we've found some good ones. Maybe you can find some more.

Make your city interesting

It sounds pretty obvious to say that nice cities are interesting to look at. But what is not so obvious (and what is important) is to find out how to make a city look interesting.

Let's start with the opposite of interesting: *boring*. Many parts of our modern cities are very boring to look at:

Housing development, Poznan, Poland

There's nothing particularly charming, exciting or lovely here. The best thing that could happen is that you'd stop noticing the buildings: You go a bit numb.

Another thing that often goes wrong in modern cities is that they start to look messy and chaotic:

Lots of different kinds of buildings are jumbled together; or there's so much advertising you can hardly see the buildings (which aren't very nice anyway); or huge, complicated roads plough their way through the city.

Yasukuni-dori, Shinjuku, Tokyo, Japan

It's helpful to think about *why* we don't like both the boring and the chaotic places.

The reason we don't like them is to do with how our brains work. Our brains are constantly searching to find patterns in things and to make sense of what's going on around us. If something is very, very simple our brains find the pattern immediately and we lose interest. It's dull and tedious.

That's why hardly anyone in the world would find this rubber bath mat fascinating to look at.

But if the pattern is too difficult to see — or if there's no pattern at all — our brains get frustrated and annoyed.

We dislike chaos because when there is not enough order and regularity we can't work out what is going on. It can make us feel lost and confused. There is an ideal point between the extremes of *too little order* and *too much order*.

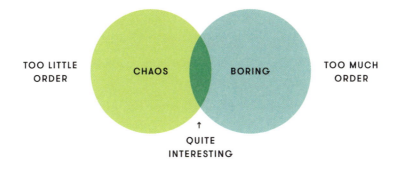

TOO LITTLE
ORDER

CHAOS

BORING

TOO MUCH
ORDER

↑
QUITE
INTERESTING

Something around the mid-point might look like this:

Robert Adam, James Adam, B. Pastorini, Ceiling in the
Countess of Derby's Dressing Room, Grosvenor Square,
London, England, 1777

At first the pattern looks obvious, but the more you look at it
the more complicated it gets. However, each complicated bit
turns out to be very ordered. When we look at this picture,
our brains are moving all the time between finding a pattern,
then feeling a bit confused, then finding another pattern.
Our brains don't get bored, but they don't get confused either.

This is interesting. In the same way that a story or a game is interesting when it is complicated enough for your brain to keep trying to work out what is happening, but it is ordered enough that you can make sense of it. It's not too complicated but it's not too simple either.

Our brains react in the same way to architecture. Here's an example of interesting architecture — a row of houses in Telč, a small town in the Czech Republic in Central Europe. The houses were all built a long time ago, in the 1600s.

Telč, Jihlava District, Czech Republic

In some ways, all the houses in this row are pretty similar. They've almost all got: three arches at the bottom, then three rectangular windows directly above the arches, then one window in the middle at the top. The top of each building is quite fancy — it's curved or stepped or pointed. So there's a background of similarity, but each house is quite individual: it has a different colour, or is highly decorated or more plain. Our brains keep on spotting patterns, but the patterns aren't simple; we keep seeing variations, but the variations make sense. The more you look the more it feels quite ordered and quite complicated at the same time.

You can use the same idea to talk about this street in London:

On the top floors of these houses, each window sits directly above the one below — but not on the ground floor, where the windows and doors have a different pattern. The bottom windows are arched, and those above have square tops, but there's a trick the architect has used: the windows on the first floor have brick arches above them, which are a bit like the arched tops of the windows below.

It takes a long time to explain all this in words, but our eyes take it in very quickly. We see that these buildings follow a pattern but we also recognise that it's a complicated pattern.

Some modern architects use the same idea in new ways:

Borneo-Sporenburg, Amsterdam, the Netherlands, 1993–1996

Overall, there's quite a strict pattern. Each house is roughly the same height and width, and the colour range is restricted to white, grey and various shades of red and brown. There are no curves — just straight lines. But within this basic pattern, each house is individual. The windows are different shapes and sizes; the materials change — some have brick, others are glass; some houses have balconies, others don't.

You can use the same idea about order and chaos to think about the layout of an entire city — like this city in England which has a slightly funny name. It's called Bath.*

Bath is a very *interesting* city to walk around. On the left of the picture you can see that the buildings make a big curve, with grass in front, then moving to the right there's a straight bit, then the houses are shaped into a circle with a very large tree in the middle. It is complicated, but it doesn't feel at all jumbled or messy, because all the buildings are quite similar.

* It really is named after a bath: a very big, outdoor one that was built there by the Romans 2,000 years ago.

They're all the same height and they're made from the same stone, so the result is a mixture of simplicity and complexity:

Bath, England

We know that beautiful cities and buildings are interesting to look at. But now we understand the recipe; we've got an idea of how to make interesting architecture:

You need to have a strong, simple pattern with plenty of variation in the details.

Become a team manager

You probably know about teams already — whether it's from sports teams, working in teams at school or watching teams on a quiz show on TV. But maybe what you haven't realised is that the idea of a 'team' is important for architecture.

Before we look at why teams are important, let's ask quite an unusual question: What actually *is* a team? A team is a group of different individuals who cooperate: They work together to do something none of them could do on their own.

Some people think that this is the greatest football team ever:

The Brazilian national football team, 1970

It's the Brazil team who played in the World Cup in 1970 (they won, of course). It's not just that they were all good players:

What made them such a great team was the way they played *together*.

They were brilliant at passing the ball very quickly, and they could anticipate what their teammates were going to do and make opportunities for each other.

You can imagine the opposite: how a group of players could fail to make a good team. They'd all be selfish, trying to keep the ball to themselves and not thinking about what anyone else was doing. The goalkeeper might suddenly run to the other end of the pitch and try to score a goal, leaving their own goal undefended. It would be a disaster.

Maybe you've noticed something about the picture of the Brazil team. There are *twelve* people in the picture — but a football team only has eleven players. There are twelve in the picture because they've included the manager, standing on the right in the light-blue top. The manager doesn't play in the match but they have a very important job:

The manager gets the players to work well together as a team.

You can use the idea of a good team and a team manager to think about architecture.

The street in this picture looks like there's no manager:

No one is in charge. Each different bit — the roads, the signs and all the buildings — is doing its own thing. They are not cooperating or helping each other. It is as if they do not even realise that there are other players on the pitch. The result is that it looks random and chaotic.

However, this isn't the only thing that goes wrong with teams. We have seen what happens when everyone does their own thing and nobody cooperates, but there's another bad version of a team which involves exactly the opposite problem. That is when the members of the team lose their individuality and become a bit robotic — the characters are very obedient and orderly, but they are not doing anything interesting. It's like they have no personality.

In football, it would be like players who only ever did exactly as they were told — they'd never have any individual flair or imagination. They'd be useless.

The architectural equivalent would be something like this: buildings that are like soulless robots.

Brandon Estate, Kennington, London, England, 1958

The whole point of a team is that as individuals we're all good at slightly different things. One person can run fast, another person keeps a cool head when things get difficult, someone else is good at scoring goals and there's another person who is particularly efficient and reliable. And if you bring all these different qualities together you get something truly amazing, something much better than any single individual could be. In a team, a group of people who are very different manage to cooperate well.

And a good team has the right mix of talented individuals cooperating together:

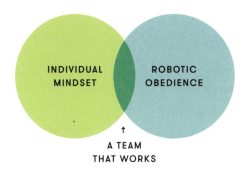

The idea of making a good team is hugely important — and not just in sport. You could say that a good family is a good team. A good friendship is a kind of team too (though it can be a team with just two people in it). And a good business depends on getting together a team of people who can work well together, even though they're all good at different things.

In architecture, good 'teams' work together to create beautiful places.

In Paris, for instance, there is a huge, wide street called the Champs-Élysées. Lots of people really like this street, though if you ask them why they think it is lovely they might not be able to tell you.

We can understand the reason why, because we are starting to realise its secret: *The buildings are a team.* All the buildings on the Champs-Élysées are a bit different, but they cooperate.

The buildings join in with each other. It's as if there's been a manager saying:

Don't run too far on your own, you need the other players to back you up; think about the opportunities you can set up for someone else; do not try to do everything yourself, you can rely on your teammates and they can rely on you.

Avenue des Champs-Élysées, Paris, France

Actually, when this part of Paris was being laid out in the 19th century there really was a person who was the team manager. It was someone called Georges-Eugène Haussmann, and he worked incredibly hard to make sure that all the different buildings played together like a great team.

One of Haussmann's best decisions as team manager was to completely reorganise the streets so that they centred around a huge arch, known as the Arc de Triomphe.

Before Haussmann came along, the arch was crowded by other buildings around it and the surrounding streets were all muddled. The arch was a great player but its teammates weren't giving it a chance to do anything. They just got in the way. What Haussmann did was get the rest of the team to cooperate with the arch. He said:

Spread out, make space for the arch.

* This arch was built in the early 1800s using a much older recipe from the Romans. It's similar to the Arch of Constantine we talked about on page 34.

In football terms the arch is like the star goal scorer — they need space to make a brilliant attack, but they also need to get lots of crosses from the other players.

As a manager, Haussmann had plenty of good ideas about how to get different streets and buildings to cooperate. One of his best tricks was to get two streets to help each other when they met at a corner.

Boulevard Haussmann, Paris, France

Instead of just joining at a sharp, abrupt angle, Haussmann made them bend into a nice curve. It's kind of like two players passing a ball beautifully to each other in a football match.

And instead of letting adverts get in the way of the buildings (which is what usually happens in cities) Haussmann made advertising hoardings that looked nice. He got them to join the team too.

Rather than using the usual boring, flat and wide advertising boards, Haussmann built attractive columns for people to stick adverts onto. He even made them look like the nearby buildings by using the same kind of metal that was used for the balconies of the houses.

He did the same with lampposts:

Avenue des Champs-Élysées, Paris, France

Haussmann thought a lot about how to make lampposts part of the team. He made them into elegant columns so that even during the day they'd be nice to look at.

Haussmann was probably the best manager of a big team of buildings there ever was. He made Paris the architectural equivalent of the 1970 Brazil football squad. Here's a picture of him (he's probably thinking about lampposts):

If Haussman was still alive, we would like to say to him:

You're our hero. Thank you from all of us.
Don't stop thinking!

Make things the right size

You already know how important it is to have things that are the right size. It's agony if a pair of shoes is too small and you could hardly walk if your shoes were ten sizes too big (you might feel a bit silly as well).

This place feels too small — though the people who live here have tried their best to make it nice:

A small bedroom in a new apartment

But this place feels too big:

Suvarnabhumi Airport, Bangkok, Thailand

Even though you're indoors you feel lost. It is quite tiring and bewildering and it's not obvious where you have to go. It's not enjoyable to be somewhere like this, and it would be strange if anyone wanted to live here.

The idea of size can help us to describe what we like and don't like in architecture.

This street is a nice size:

Altstadt, Freiburg im Breisgau, Germany

This street is in the town of Freiburg im Breisgau in the South of Germany. The houses on either side are not too high, the road is made of stones (rather than asphalt) and it's designed for people to walk along rather than for cars.

The buildings aren't too close to each other across the street, either, but they are close enough so it feels cosy. It's just the right size.

But this street, in New South Wales in Australia, is too wide:

The buildings on the side of this incredibly wide street look lonely and almost forgotten. If you walk along the road all you will see is dark grey asphalt, which isn't a very attractive material. If this place could speak to you it would only talk about cars and buses and parking. Oddly, it doesn't actually need to be so big: This is a small town and there isn't a huge amount of traffic.

This square in Rome is a lovely size:

It's called Piazza Mattei (the word *piazza* means 'town square' in Italian — be careful not to mix it up with pizza, which is also very nice but for very different reasons). This square's on a *human scale*, because its size fits with the ways our bodies work. If you were on one side and you saw your friend walking past on the other side you could call to them and they would hear you. But you can be private too: If you were in one corner having a conversation, someone in another corner wouldn't be able to overhear what you were saying. If you were playing in the middle of the square and your mum or dad was looking out of a window on the third floor they would be able to see if you were OK.

But some squares are too big:

Alexanderplatz, Berlin, Germany

This square in Berlin is called Alexanderplatz (*platz* is German for 'town square'). It's huge, shapeless and uninviting. If you were in the middle, the buildings would feel really far away. If you saw a friend on the other side, you wouldn't be able to get their attention. If someone was looking out of a window and you were in the middle of the square you would not see the expression on their face.

Being on a human scale means that spaces and buildings feel like they were designed to fit in with our bodies.

In the past it was very difficult to make really big buildings. People did not have huge cranes or steel to work with, and they had not worked out how to make strong materials like concrete. They also did not have elevators: They only came into widespread use at the beginning of the 20th century, so before then the height of buildings was limited by how many stairs people could climb.

Hardly any buildings for people to live or work in were more than five stories high. It was only very special buildings like churches, towers, theatres or castles that were higher. So, in terms of height, most towns had to be on a human scale.

Bruges, Belgium

This is Bruges, which is in Belgium. The old centre of the city was built well before 1900 and it hasn't changed much since.

All the houses and offices and shops are fairly low — four or five stories high at most. A few special buildings (mostly churches) can be seen clearly above them.

Rozenhoedkaai, Bruges, Belgium

A lot of people think that this old part of Bruges is one of the most attractive places in all of Europe.

Today, it's easy to make gigantic buildings. So, lots of places end up feeling like they are squashing us.

This is New York. It was built with cars and elevators in mind:

New York, USA

The busy street is much too long to walk up and down and the buildings are so high that if you are standing on the pavement you can hardly see the tops of the tower blocks on either side.

There's nothing wrong with buildings being big. What matters is *why* they are big.

Let's think about something very big that probably looks like it hasn't got anything at all to do with architecture.

Saturn V and Apollo 11, Kennedy Space Centre, Florida, USA, 1969

On 16th July 1969 this rocket, called Saturn V, was launched from the Kennedy Space Centre in Florida. In a tiny pod at the top were the astronauts who would soon become the very first people to land on the moon. The rocket is enormous (look at the yellow crane next to it), but it also stands for an enormous idea. It's saying:

We can do really difficult but wonderful things.
We can explore and understand the universe.

The rocket was big, but the idea behind the rocket was even bigger. Something big is great when it stands for a great idea.

This can happen in architecture too. Back in the 1870s the University of Glasgow decided to build a huge new tower and spire that would rise high above their old buildings. Here it is:

The Gilbert Scott Building, Glasgow, Scotland, 1870–1891

They wanted to build something very big and tall that could be seen by everyone. The tower was designed to tell everyone who lived in the city about what the university was for. It said:

We believe in education and we think it is very important to understand the past, learn new things and find out about science. We don't just think this is good for us, we think this is good for everyone.

It was a hugely important message and so it made sense to have a huge building to beam it out to the world.

Or what about this example?

Thomas Hosmer Shepherd, St Paul's Cathedral, 1829–1831

This enormous church, with its lovely dome, was built in London in the 1600s after the Great Fire of London burnt down the one that stood there before. It took over 35 years to build and everyone in London helped pay for it. It's called St Paul's Cathedral. It's so large that all the people who lived in the middle of the city could fit inside it. It was always open and anyone could go in and spend as long as they liked there.

St Paul's Cathedral is designed to tell everyone some really good things. When it speaks, it says:

It's important that you think about the meaning of your life and feel sorry when you've been unkind to others; don't just think about money and work — think about beauty as well.

Even if you were miles away you could see the dome and the towers — and its message would always reach you. It was making a very big collective statement:

This is what we think matters. It's great that this building is so big because it's got such lovely big ideas behind it.

For nearly 300 years St Paul's Cathedral continued to be by far the highest and most impressive building in the whole of London. But then things changed.

The London skyline, England

It became so easy to build enormous buildings, they could be built for any reason at all. In fact, not too long ago a much, much bigger new tower called the Shard was built close to the old dome of St Paul's. The new tower is utterly enormous, but it does not have a good message to send us. It is mainly filled with offices for businesses that sell oil or move money around the world or (weirdly) help other businesses find offices in other buildings. There are also some apartments and a hotel inside.

The Shard, London, England, 2009

The ideas that this tower stands for are not important. It would be crazy to say:

Listen very carefully, we have got an amazing idea that everyone needs to pay attention to: businesses should rent office space and people should live in apartments.

But, sadly, that is the message this building is sending. It's got a very loud voice but it's saying very boring things. In fact, the main reason it's so big is so that the owners can say:

We've got the biggest building.

That might be exciting for them, but it isn't terribly exciting for anyone else — since it's their building, not ours. It's sad that this selfish message now has a much bigger and louder voice than the kindly old dome. The new tower is a bit of a bully: it uses its very big size to stop other buildings talking.

Some big buildings, however, are wonderful because they look beautiful. Some of the very nicest ones are in New York.

San Remo apartments, New York, USA, 1931

These towers in New York start out quite wide at the bottom, gradually get narrower as they go up and then end with a spire that points into the sky.

Chrysler Building, New York, USA, 1930

Empire State Building, New York, USA, 1930

They look a bit like magnificent rockets ready to blast off into outer space.

When buildings are huge and beautiful at the same time, they are beaming out a much more interesting message:

Beauty is important.

And they're being generous. The buildings say:

We know you don't live or work in us, but we want you to have a nice time looking at us, so we have gone to a lot of trouble to make sure we have lovely shapes.

The bigger something is, the more important it is that it looks nice. Otherwise we might end up with places like this:

Kin Ming Estate, Tiu Keng Wan, Hong Kong, China, 2003

Now we can understand the problem a bit better. It's not bad that some buildings are big: It's bad that they are very big and not saying anything interesting or meaningful. Realising this helps to confirm the next step in our architectural recipe:

If you want to make a building big, make sure it has something genuinely lovely and significant to say.

Woolworth Building, New York, USA, 1912

Use nice materials

When you're building a city, you've got the option to use all kinds of different materials: brick, stone, wood, steel, glass, concrete. One of the things that makes the biggest difference to how nice (or horrible) a place or a building looks is the quality of the materials you use. Here's an example:

Seeley Historical Library, University of Cambridge, Cambridge, England, 1964–1968

In this building the bricks look grubby and cheap and harsh. Sadly, this is the history library at the University of Cambridge in England. It is terrible that such an important place looks so horrible.

When you are looking at this you might think that brick isn't a very nice material. Maybe if we want lovely buildings we've got to avoid using bricks. But that can't be right, because sometimes brick can look quite wonderful:

Bötzow Brewery, Berlin, Germany, 2019

This building is also made of brick, but it is more attractive. The thing is, there are actually lots of different kinds of brick. In this building, the brick is a pale, delicate colour and there are lots of little variations between the individual bricks. It looks surprisingly soft, but the structure also looks very strong. It feels clean, warm and gentle.

We can look closely at bricks to understand the difference:

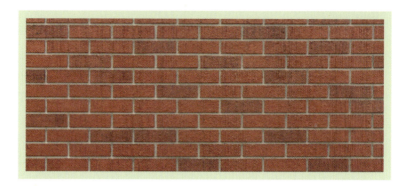

These bricks have straight and sharp edges and the surface of each brick is very flat, so the wall lacks texture. The colour varies a bit but it's not a very appealing pattern. If this wall was a person they might be quite boring and unimaginative; they wouldn't be good at telling a story or making up a game.

These bricks vary quite a lot; the edges and surfaces aren't precise. It looks like it could be interesting to touch. If this wall was a person they'd probably do slightly unexpected, but intriguing, things. They would not just be obsessed with one thing — they might be quite keen on science, but they'd also like playing hide-and-seek; they might like reading, but they'd be great at having pillow fights as well.

So we can't just say that all brick is bad — but we can't say the opposite either. It's neither always horrible, nor always lovely. It depends on which kind of brick is used and how it is used.

You can see the same thing happening with other materials. Take concrete. Suppose you came across this building:

Apollo Pavilion, Peterlee, England, 1969

You might think concrete is pretty awful. The architect, Victor Pasmore, has used some interesting shapes but the material looks grimy and a bit miserable.

Unfortunately, this concrete pavilion is situated in the middle of England where it rains a lot and there are not many sunny days. That's not particularly good for concrete. When it gets wet, concrete gets stained — and when the sun isn't shining it looks drab and lifeless.

But concrete *can* look splendid in other conditions.

Salk Institute for Biological Studies, La Jolla, California, USA, 1965

This building is part of a science research institute in La Jolla, California. It doesn't rain much here and it's sunny nearly all the time. Here the concrete looks monumental and serene: solid and yet strangely light.

Let's look at some details:

Rain and dirt streaked concrete

If this concrete wall was a person they would always be in a grumpy mood. If you wanted to go on a picnic they'd say no because it would probably rain; if you wanted to play a card game they'd say they did not feel like it; if you were feeling happy they would point out a pimple on your nose.

Rammed concrete, Bruder Klaus Field Chapel, Mechernich, Germany, 2007

Here the pattern on the concrete is gentle and delicate. If this concrete was a person, they would be quite quiet, but they'd be sensitive and thoughtful. They'd notice things that other people might not — the unusual shape of a cloud, maybe, or the nice design of the wheel arch on a car. If you were feeling awkward about something they would pick up on it and try to put you at ease. They'd be patient if you tried to tell them something complicated.

So, just like brick, we can't just say definitively that concrete is horrible or that concrete is lovely. It just depends on exactly what kind of concrete you use and where you use it.

Even a material you might think would be quite terrible for building — like plastic — can be used nicely. Mostly it isn't, though. You might have come across a building like this:

Modern warehouse, Rotterdam, the Netherlands

The surface of this red and black building looks dull and a bit sticky, like the skin of an unwashed apple. It wouldn't be nice to touch it. It does not have much personality: it is bland and unresponsive. If you told it a joke it would just stare at you.

But this building uses plastic in an attractive way:

The Chesapeake Boathouse, Oklahoma City, Oklahoma, USA, 2006

Light can shine through the panels — they can be lit up from the inside at night, creating a lovely soft glow. Using very tall, thin strips creates an elegant pattern. It's sophisticated but warm, like a fashionable, but very kindly, aunt.

Traditionally, marble is the most prestigious building material. It is not hard to understand why. Marble is an extremely strong and long-lasting stone and it often has lovely patterns (called 'veins') running through it.

This lovely green marble wall is in one of the most famous buildings of the 20th century — the Barcelona Pavilion, built between 1928 and 1929 in the city of Barcelona, Spain (hence the name). The pavilion was designed by a German architect called Ludwig Mies van der Rohe.

The green marble slab looks extremely heavy and permanent — as if it could last forever — but it's also beautiful. Marble is lovely to touch; on a hot day it's blissful to lean your forehead against its smooth, cool surface.

But even marble can be badly used.

An ornate marble staircase

This staircase is showing off — it thinks it is wonderful but actually it's not all that attractive. The steps look messy and don't go with the floor; the half-columns at the bottom look stumpy. The marble itself might be quite nice if you could take it out and use it to make something better, like a worktop in a kitchen, but here it's rather depressing. It reminds us of someone who goes around boasting all the time.

And, finally, what about wood? Wood can be one of the most appealing building materials.

But it isn't always delightful:

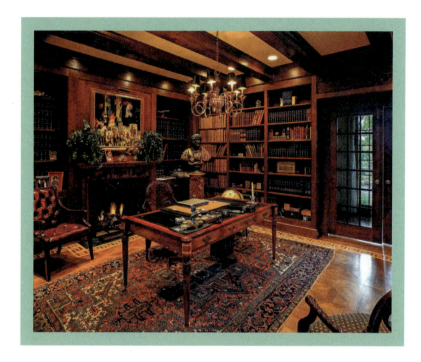

A wood panelled office

In this room, part of the problem is that all the wood has been highly polished; it looks like plastic. It's trying to be fancy but ends up looking heavy and oppressive. The huge beams in the ceiling feel like they are pressing down on your head. If you were having a conversation with this room it would tell you very long, boring stories about itself. It would be ages before you could get a word in.

However, the next wooden room, designed by Peter Zumthor, feels clean and simple — it would be a very calm and cosy place to sleep in.

The light colour of the wood works well with the view (there's usually snow on the tops of the mountains outside).

The Unterhus, Zumthor Vacation Homes, Leis, Switzerland, 2009

Here the wood feels closer to its natural state: It's a reminder of the trees and forests from which it came, and that surround the building. If this room could speak, it would have quite a cheerful voice; maybe it wouldn't say very much, but it would listen sweetly to whatever you had to say. It would be nodding a lot to the mountains outside.

The lesson here is that there is not one particular kind of material that's automatically better than another.

Rather, there are good and bad versions of pretty much every material you can think of using for building. Once you start thinking about material (and looking at different materials more closely) you start to develop your own preferences. You become more sensitive to, and precise about, what it is you really like.

For example, maybe you quite like wooden floors. This one could look OK:

Glossy laminate wood floors

But it's not as nice as this:

Unvarnished natural wood floors

So, instead of just saying that you simply like wooden floors, you could say:

I like natural wood floorboards that are quite light
in colour and aren't too waxy or highly polished.

Of course, you are probably not going to be saying that very often — but if you were designing a house it would be a good thing to know.

It's the same with all the other materials you'll be using when, one day perhaps, you build your city. You will be able to say:

We need bricks, but they have to be the right bricks,
or we can use concrete, but only in some places.

Or:

Yes, it would be great to have some marble,
but we need to be careful how we use it.

You'll be saying:

I know plastic sounds awful, but if
we are clever we can make it lovely.

You'll be having some very interesting conversations.

Develop a local style

Some things are pretty much the same all around the world. A tin opener in Iceland looks like a tin opener in Morocco; a fridge in Brazil is a lot like a fridge in Australia; and quite similar models of car are popular in Japan and Turkey. There are some people who think this is what should happen with buildings, too. If technology works all around the world, why shouldn't we have the same buildings everywhere?

One of the first people who thought this way was Le Corbusier. Back in the 1930s, Le Corbusier began making drawings and models of what he thought cities could look like in the future.

Le Corbusier, plans for La Ville Radieuse (The Radiant City), 1924

He wrote a book in which he argued that all the cities in the world should look like his drawings. It might sound madly ambitious, but lots and lots of architects actually did read his book and used his ideas.

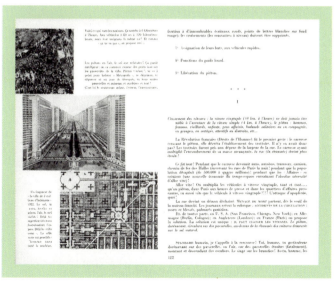

Le Corbusier, plans for La Ville Radieuse (The Radiant City), 1924

Huge developments based on Le Corbusier's book were built in Russia and America:

Kalinin Avenue, Moscow, Russia, 1962–1968

Co-op City development, the Bronx, New York, USA, 1966–1973

In the United Kingdom:

The Sentinels tower blocks, Birmingham, England, 1967–1971

And South Korea:

Banpo Xi apartment complex, Seoul, South Korea, 2008

And in India:

Apartment blocks in Chennai, India, 2009

This is a tiny selection from many thousands of similar developments that were built in practically every country.

Cities in very different parts of the world started to look the same. Sometimes you might look up at a building and have no idea where you might be. You could be anywhere.

Is it bad if everywhere looks the same?

To answer this question, let's look at some old buildings that are very different *because they are in different places.*

We'll start our exploration in Switzerland.

This is a special kind of house that was built for centuries in Switzerland: It's called a chalet. You might think that the Swiss built houses like this just because it looks pretty, but actually the way the chalet was designed depended on the local conditions.

Look at the huge, steep roof that juts right out in front of the house. They did that because they get lots and lots of snow in the winter. If the roof was flat the snow would build up very quickly and get so heavy that it might crush the whole house. The sloping roof helps all the snow slide off, and if the roof didn't stick out, the snow would fall right onto the balcony and build up against the walls.

The chalet is made out of wood because there are plenty of trees nearby, and they put in a balcony and lots of windows because they wanted to enjoy the view of the mountains.

Now look at these houses in Morocco, in North Africa. They look totally different. Why do you think that is?

Aït Benhaddou, Morocco

The houses have flat roofs because it hardly ever rains here and it will never snow. You do not need to worry about how the rain will drain off or about heavy snow building up. The houses are made of brick: They used brick because there were not many trees, so they could not get wood. Their bricks are made of dried clay as it was easy to dry the clay in the hot sunshine. The houses have small windows because keeping the interior cool was more important than letting in light.

Long ago, in Norway, the Vikings built houses like this:

Landa Park, Forsand, Norway

The roof was made of very thick layers of woven grass — there was a lot of grass around — and the thick walls were made of piled up earth, which is very good for keeping out the cold. They only had a few tiny windows (and sometimes none at all) because they didn't want the heat to escape and because a lot of the time there wasn't much to look at anyway (in Norway it is dark for a lot of the year). This kind of house is called a *longhouse* — because it's very long, obviously! They needed to be long because lots of people lived in them: not just the parents and children, but also the grandparents and cousins and nephews and nieces.

Let's look at a house in Spain, built hundreds of years ago:

The Court of the Lions, The Alhambra, Granada, Spain, c. 1362–1391

The house is built around a courtyard with a fountain in the middle. The jets of water help to keep the air cool during the hot summer. There is an open colonnade around the edge of the courtyard so that you can stay in the shade when walking between different parts of the building. The columns are very thin — they look a bit like the trunks of palm trees, because palms were the favourite trees of the people who lived here. The house doesn't have windows on the outside: all the rooms look onto the courtyard. That's because people worried about having nosey neighbours.

From all of these examples we can see that different styles of buildings connect with the different ways that people like to live. They're connected to the local weather, to the landscape and to the materials that are locally available.

Each building tells a story about who lives there and what they care about.

Every different kind of building shows what that particular place, and the life of the people who live there, is like. This is what makes these buildings *meaningful*.

Now we can see what's going wrong when the same buildings are built everywhere. The buildings stop telling us anything about the place they were built and the people who live there. They stop being meaningful.

More recently, some architects have tried to make modern buildings that also have a local feel, and which can tell us important stories about where they are and how they are adapted to the local conditions.

One interesting example comes from Australia. A lot of the houses that are built in Australia could really be anywhere.

Front elevation of a new modern Australian home

You can find houses that look pretty much just like this in California and in England and in Germany and in Canada.

But a little while ago, a great Australian architect called Glenn Murcutt decided to design a house for himself. One thing he did was to place big water tanks in full view. He made them out of a nice, bright material — he did not try to hide them away. Water tanks are very important in this part of Australia because it does not rain very much at all, so if you want to water your garden — or even have a deep bath — you need to supply your own water.

The shape of the house is a bit like a sheep-shearing barn, which is also meaningful, because the economy of this area is based on sheep, and so there are lots of barns nearby for shearing the wool.

Glenn Murcutt, Kangaroo Valley House, New South Wales, Australia

The house has large windows which open completely so the inside and outside feel easily connected, which is great here because the evenings are warm for nine months of the year. The water tanks, and the shape of the house and the big window are saying:

This house is in a very specific place — a place that's not at all like many other parts of the world.

Now let's look at another example of how a building can be connected to where it is. In the German city of Berlin there are lots of museums. One of the most impressive things you can see there are the remains of an ancient Greek temple:

It has a huge flight of steps that slopes up in the middle and two high wings with columns that come forward at each side.

Recently, the museum wanted to build an extension. And the architect, David Chipperfield, had a clever idea: they'd make the new building echo the design of the most famous exhibit. This new building is a modern version of something familiar. It has columns and steps — just like the big exhibit — but the columns feel contemporary because they are square rather than round and much slimmer.

The building looks at home here, but it's not an exact copy. It is speaking about where it is, and why it is the way it is, but it's got a modern voice.

James Simon Galerie, Museum Island, Berlin, Germany, 1999–2019

You can see another example of this idea in one of the world's oldest cities: Jerusalem. The city of Jerusalem has probably been inhabited for 4,000 years, maybe longer.

In this city, there is a rule that new buildings have to use the same, traditional kind of stone as the old buildings, like the stone used for this building, which is one of the old gates to the city (the city used to have a wall all the way around it).

Damascus Gate, Jerusalem, Israel, 1537

Not that long ago, when a new town hall was being built, the architect used the same kind of stone:

Jerusalem Historical City Hall Building, Jerusalem, Israel, 1930

They also built towers on either side of the entrance, a bit like the old gate. Now the town hall isn't just a building that could be anywhere — it makes sense that it is here.

Next, let's jump around the globe and land on the big island that sits next to India: Sri Lanka. In Colombo, the capital city of Sri Lanka, the government needed to build a new parliament building. It's always a big decision for a country: What should the main building of the government look like?

Everyone wanted the building to look modern, but they also wanted it to look like it really belonged. First, the architects looked carefully at a very old, traditional building called the Royal Audience Hall:

Audience Hall, Royal Palace of Kandy, Kandy, Sri Lanka. 1783–1875

Hundreds of years ago, the king used to have important meetings to discuss how to run the country in this hall.

Having looked at this important old building, the architect, who was called Geoffrey Bawa, developed a modern version that was influenced by the traditional design.

The New Sri Lanka Parliament, Sri Jayawardenepura Kotte, Colombo, Sri Lanka, 1979–1982

First, they used the same kind of roof, which has quite a shallow slope at the bottom but then gets steeper. They also used lots of columns, but they made them out of concrete rather than wood.

136

With these design elements, the building is saying something important. It is saying:

I'm interested in, and loyal to, the past and I don't want to forget where I've come from. But I'm also interested in what we can do now (and in what we can maybe do tomorrow). You don't have to decide between past or present: You can like both at the same time.

You can see something similar happening in a building called the Independence Palace in Hồ Chí Minh City, once the home of the president of a country called South Vietnam.

Independence Palace, Hồ Chí Minh City, Vietnam, 1962–1966

This government building was built in the 1960s, and like the parliament building in Colombo, it is both interested in the modern world while also feeling nicely connected to the past.

The front of the palace is a blend of old and new. There is a row of thin concrete columns holding up a flat roof — that's the kind of design you will find on many modern buildings.

But look in between the columns:

In between each modern column the architect has inserted twelve smaller posts, in three rows of four. The idea of having posts in between columns wasn't actually anything new.

In fact, it was an old idea in Vietnam. You can see a simpler version of the same idea in a very old Vietnamese house:

Cham House, Vietnamese Museum of Ethnology, Hanoi, Vietnam

So, although the Independence Palace is obviously a modern building, it is also traditional. That means it truly belongs where it is. We have found another recipe:

People like buildings to look like they remember the past — but also look ready for the future.

Make the city lively

Before the 20th century, cities were much, much smaller than they are today. This is a map of London from a couple of hundred years ago:

John Rocque, Map of London, 1741-1745

London was one of the biggest cities in the world at that time, but you could walk from one side to the other in around an hour — as long as you didn't dawdle in front of shop windows or stop to chat to your friends. This meant that even if you were right in the middle, it wouldn't take long to get to the farms, fields and woods in the countryside.

Cities had to be small because the only way to get around for most people was by walking (or running if you were in a hurry). And because they were small, everything and everyone was jumbled close together. Lots of streets looked like this:

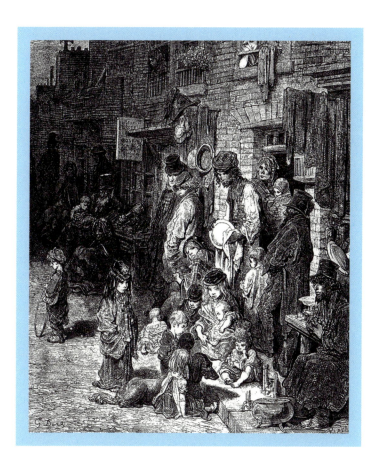

Gustave Doré, Wentworth Street, Whitechapel, 1872

If you lived in this street, there might be a furniture shop next door and a small factory making glass bottles with some flats above it nearby, and maybe a shop selling beer or bread at the other end of the street. Around the corner you'd see people making things out of metal or sawing pieces of wood. People mostly worked very close to where they lived, and knew their neighbours and local shopkeepers. You would see the same people all the time, and you would hear them gossiping and arguing, so you'd find out all about their lives. It could be very interesting, but you would not get much privacy. The streets would often be dirty and congested and every time you went out the door there would be a crowd of people. It could feel quite overwhelming.

Then everything changed.

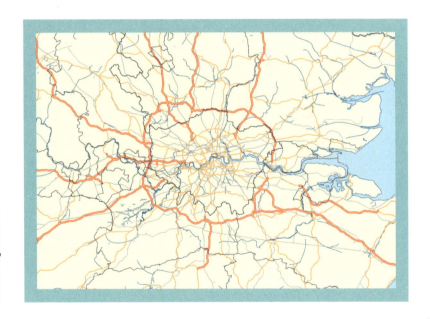

London, England, 2020

This is a map of London today. The old London that we were just thinking about could easily fit into the small, dark orange sort-of-circle in the middle.

It would take you a whole (very, very tiring) day to walk from one side to the other. And you'd have to walk fast all the time.

The reason that cities have grown so big is transport. Railway lines and underground trains, big roads and cars and buses mean you can live ten or twenty or thirty miles away from the city centre. Once modern transport came along, most people moved away from the old, crowded city centres. They went to live in the *suburbs*.

A typical British suburb

Millions of streets a bit like this were built all over the world. In fact, in many countries more than half the population lives in suburbs.

The nice thing about suburbs is that they are cleaner and quieter and you can have a lot more space to yourself. But it turns out that there are some serious problems too. The suburbs can be too quiet. You might go out of your door and not see anyone at all in the street. There might not be any shops nearby — or cafes or restaurants. In fact, a lot of these places are called 'dormitory suburbs' — places where people just stay at home and sleep.

Shops are concentrated in distant shopping centres and retail parks, with huge, ugly car parks in front of them:

Lakeside Retail Park, Grays, England

144

Most people no longer live anywhere near where they work. Factories and warehouses are kept out of the suburbs and instead they're grouped together in dreary industrial zones, like this one in Spain:

Only the people who work there ever spend any time in them. It means we don't get to see how the world works. They might be making aeroplane wings or submarines or your favourite kind of biscuits — but you will never know because it is all hidden away.

Lots of other people still work in the middle of cities, but because hardly anyone actually lives there a lot of streets are dominated by big anonymous office blocks.

This street is near the middle of London, a ginormous city, but no one would enjoy walking along it. We have no idea what's going on behind the concrete and glass walls. It could be very interesting: People could be deciding how to increase the number of bees in the countryside or working out how to make it easier to learn a foreign language, or they could be making films about what life was like in the Middle Ages, but because you'll never go there, you'll never feel part of it.

The new way of organising things — with dormitory suburbs, distant shopping centres, hidden away factories and boring streets lined with offices — is a disaster. Nobody lives near all the places they have to go, so we end up having to spend a lot of our time commuting. (Many, many adults say that commuting is the most annoying and frustrating part of everyday life.)

This way of living makes us feel isolated and a lot of people get lonely.

But don't worry, there's an interesting alternative:

A lively, compact city.

If we were to make a diagram of how to make a city that is lively and compact, and doesn't feel too overwhelming or too boring, it would look something like this:

TOO CROWDED   OPPRESSIVE   BORING   TOO SPREAD OUT

↑
LIVELY
AND COMPACT

Let's see what this looks like. On this lively street there are little shops, cafes and restaurants:

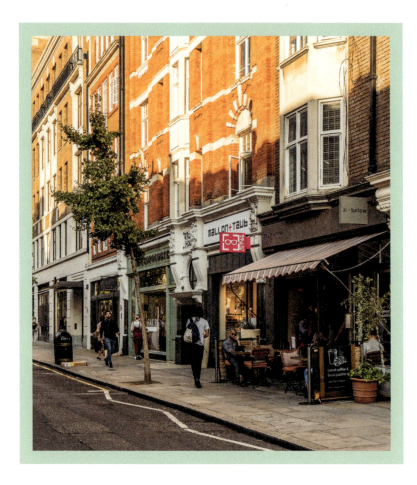

Marylebone High Street, Marylebone, London, England

On this street there is a bookshop, a florist and a shop selling things like ironing boards and kettles; then a clothes shop, a greengrocers and also a burger bar and a place that sells racing bikes. On the upper floors there are some offices but also plenty of flats; so there are always people around.

If you live here you can see people at work, look them in the eye as they walk down the road and feel connected to them. These are the kinds of streets most people like.

West End Lane, West Hampstead, London, England

The problem is that there just aren't enough of these kinds of streets. We got to the wrong idea:

We thought we wanted suburbs but what we really wanted was liveliness.

There is another really important idea that can help keep cities lively. A city needs all kinds of service buildings to keep it functioning, such as factories, banks, railway terminals, water pumping stations and shopping centres. We've come to take it for granted that these things are always horrible to look at. We can't imagine them being part of what makes a city look nice, so we keep them far away from where we live. Nowadays we think it would be horrible to live next door to a huge factory or a big railway station or beside a shopping centre. If the government said they were going to build a water pumping station next to where you live, you'd probably think that was terrible. All these things are part of the life of a city, but because they're usually so ugly we try to hide them away — and the result is that cities come to feel lifeless.

But this isn't necessary at all. In the past, people were proud of their service buildings and tried to make them as lovely as possible. Banks were often the nicest buildings. This building in Edinburgh was originally the headquarters of a bank:

The Old Bank of Scotland Building, Edinburgh, Scotland, 1800–1806

It looked so nice that it was not a problem to have this huge office block right in the middle of the city — in fact, it makes the city look even better.

Railway companies wanted stations to look magnificent, too.

Grand Central Terminal, New York, USA, 1903-1913

This is the entrance to one of the busiest railway stations in the world, Grand Central Terminal in New York, but it looks calm and elegant.

Cities were proud of having clean drinking water and they wanted their pumping stations to show how they felt, so they built beautiful ones, like this:

The Fergusson Gallery, Perth, Scotland, 1832

It's hard to believe now but this delicate and pretty building originally housed the machines that kept water flowing into people's kitchens and bathrooms. It's in the centre of a city (Perth, in Scotland) and people love it because it's beautiful.

In this city people say:

I'm trying to get a flat near the pumping station
but it's difficult because obviously everyone wants
to live in that part of town.

It's sad that today we can hardly imagine building a water
pumping station that is so nice that people would want to
live right next to it.

As well as banks, stations and pumping stations, in the past
some factory owners wanted their factories to be fascinating
and beautiful. This large building is the Templeton Carpet
Factory in Glasgow (now called Templeton on the Green).

Templeton on the Green, Glasgow, Scotland, 1889–1892

It looks a little like a palace, but it was built as a factory for making (you guessed it) carpets. It's in the middle of the city, next to a park. Today we'd think it was completely awful to have a factory next to a park. But because the owner made sure this factory was beautiful it actually makes the city look nicer. Lots of people go to the park just because they want to see this building.

Even shopping centres were designed to look magnificent. This one is so lovely that people are delighted that it's in the centre of their city:

Galleria Vittorio Emanuele II, Milan, Italy, 1865–1877

Making factories, office buildings, shopping centres and stations lovely means they can be close to where people live.

You do not need to push them away into distant, dull places. You can keep all the life and activity in the city. This is a great way to live, but mostly we don't get the chance because we've forgotten to make service buildings nice. We do not have to make this mistake: we can work with an idea:

Make all functional buildings beautiful.

There's another, unexpected benefit of small, lively cities: Compact cities use up much less energy. If you live near to where you work, you might not need a car and you certainly won't need so much petrol. You may even be able to walk to work instead of taking the bus. It is much more efficient to keep a compact city flat cool in summer and warm in winter than it is to heat and cool a large house in the suburbs. You might not have thought about it before, but good architecture and lively cities are an important part of the solution to one of the world's most difficult questions: *how to use less energy.*

This is a really important point. When we worry about climate change it's tempting to see cities as the enemy. But actually, it's certain kinds of cities that we have to worry about. If we really wanted to, we could build cities that are beautiful and much more energy efficient. We're not going to be able to get rid of cities — that's impossible. But if we make cities lovely and lively we can directly reduce their carbon footprint. It's a strange but hugely important thought:

Beauty might be the key to saving the planet.

Repetition is good

One of the unfortunate things that happened to architecture towards the end of the 20th century was the emergence of the idea that every new building should look unique. Architects began to think that new buildings should look different from any other building. This has resulted in some very strange things being built...

20 Fenchurch Street ('The Walkie-Talkie'), London, England, 2010–2014

This building in London is called the 'walkie-talkie', because it has the same sort of shape as an old-fashioned phone.

'The Walkie-Talkie', London, England, 2010–2014

A Walkie-Talkie phone

PRESS-TO-TALK SWITCH NOT DEPRESSED WHILE RECEIVING

It's true, no one had ever before thought of making a gigantic version of an old mobile phone... The building is unique, but it's also rather weird, because it's as if it's loudly broadcasting a slightly unhinged message:

Pay attention everyone! We should all be thinking
about military field telephones from the 1940s.
Honestly, I am really, really serious about this.
If you live or work around here I'm going to remind
you every single day. I'm not going to let you forget.
Never!

Or what about this:

The Longaberger Company ('Big Basket'), Newark, Ohio, USA, 1997

This building is saying:

We believe in baskets! We love baskets.
We love them so much we want to live and
work in a big orange basket. Baskets forever!

It's deeply unusual to want to make a building that's exactly
like a basket. Of course it's unique. And perhaps it makes you
giggle for a moment. But a joke is really only funny once and
a building has to be used for a long, long time. Seeing this
building every day would be like hearing someone tell exactly

the same joke again and again for years. It might have been amusing once, but after a month you'd be getting desperate.

The problem is that making buildings that look very unusual isn't connected to what people generally like about cities. The cities we love and want to visit usually have lots of buildings that look quite similar. They were designed by people who were happy to repeat a good idea that had already been tried and tested and shown to work well. They weren't interested in making novelty buildings.

Take these houses in London, for instance:

Terraced houses built in the 18th century

This kind of building has been popular for 200 years. The person who designed it didn't think about how to make buildings unique — they just followed a pattern that was already very well established: they copied the design from a recipe book. Often we think copying is a bad idea but, in architecture, it's a good idea to follow the recipe.

A recipe is the best way of confidently making attractive streets and cities.

Here's the relevant page from the recipe book the architect used. (The houses aren't exactly the same as in the recipe, but they're pretty similar.)

Georgian architectural drawings

This recipe book was written in the 18th century by the British government at the time.

The government looked around and found the kinds of houses that most people really liked, and then they said:

We know what works, let's repeat it.

The recipe book explained just what you needed to do — it showed what houses of various sizes should look like, what kinds of doors and windows and roofs to have. Then they made a law that every architect had to follow these recipes.

Georgian terraced houses, Bath, England

These rules worked very nicely. Whole streets were built in a similar way, so they looked harmonious. But because you could make little changes, the buildings don't all look exactly the same. Today these streets are still very popular.

In this London street, they changed the recipe very slightly and painted the ground-floor walls white.

Packington Street, Islington, London, England

In this one they gave all the windows a slight curve at the top.

Westminster, London, England

And here they made the street into a lovely crescent and used stone instead of brick — but they were still basically following the same rules.

The Circus, Bath, England, 1754–1768

Around the world there are lots of different and very good recipes and each of them has been used many, many times.

For example, in Paris, for a long time there was a clear recipe for making apartment buildings:

Thousands and thousands of apartment buildings all over Paris were constructed using this recipe.

STEP ONE

Put shops on the ground floor.

STEP TWO

Add an in-between storey immediately above them.
This is for storage for the shops or for offices.

STEP THREE

Above that you must use pale-coloured stone.

STEP FOUR

Above the shops and offices put an iron balcony
that goes all the way round.

STEP FIVE

On the next two floors don't use long balconies,
just have little ones right in front of each window.

STEP SIX

Make the windows tall: they have to open right
down to the floor, just like doors do.

STEP SEVEN

Put another long balcony near the top.

STEP EIGHT

Add a grey roof with attic windows in it.

Congratulations! You've built a really nice apartment block, just like this one:

Practically everyone agrees that Paris is a lovely city, but not many people understand that it's because the architects used a good recipe!

In the city of Bern, Switzerland, you can see a different recipe that was used for making streets. The main part of this recipe is to have a big, wide arcade at street level, so if it's very sunny you can keep cool and if it's raining you can keep dry.

You have to make sure the arcade is really nice:

To do that, you can put interesting shops, and plenty of cafes and restaurants along it. Give it a curved ceiling, because that makes it feel airy and special. Then you build some flats and some offices above it — not too high though, just three stories (maybe sometimes you could add one more).

This recipe was used in many old cities.

Place Saint-Louis, Metz, France

In this one they put the arcade next to an open square, where they have markets at the weekend.

Here they added some special bay windows (that jut out into the street) above the arcade where you can look at the street.

Piazza della Mostra (Muster square), Bolzano, Italy

The secret for making lovely places is to use the recipes that we already know work well. You do not have to worry about coming up with an idea no one has ever had before. Instead what you need to do is think about the next step in our recipe for a beautiful city:

Find places you really like and ask yourself: *What's the recipe here?*

Then use the recipe you have discovered to make lots more houses and towns and cities that will be lovely too.

Conclusion

Why are houses so expensive?

We are almost at the end of our exploration into the whys and hows of architecture. But before we say goodbye, there's a few more big questions we'd like to consider.

Why are houses so expensive? This question seems to bother pretty much everyone (even people who are not especially interested in architecture), because at some point nearly all of us will need to rent or want to buy somewhere to live. But unfortunately, in many countries houses and apartments are very expensive.

Painted Ladies, San Francisco, USA

If we ask why houses are so expensive the answer might not be what you expect. It's not actually the buildings that cost so much money: The thing that pushes up the price of houses is the land that they are built on. It's puzzling because there is obviously a lot of land around.

The picture below was taken from the window of a plane, just before it landed in a big, crowded and expensive city. As you can see, there's a huge amount of land with almost no houses and no towns or villages. Why not build a new city here?

River Tweed, Scottish Borders, Scotland

The reason is that you're not allowed to. In many countries there's just a tiny amount of land where you are allowed to build anything new, so the price of land becomes very high.

So, let's ask the next question: Why aren't we allowed to build on all the empty land? It's because most people think it is a bad idea to dig up a nice area of the countryside, like this:

North Yorkshire, UK

And build something like this:

Braehead shopping centre, Renfrew, Glasgow, 1999

Or turn it into something like this:

Markham, Ontario, Canada

That makes a lot of sense. It's a real pity that houses cost so much, but maybe that's better than ruining the countryside. That's how plenty of people think.

Your brain might be getting a bit tired by now, but let's ask just one more question — it's the most important one:

Is it really buildings that people object to?

Do we want to preserve the countryside (and keep houses very expensive) because we hate buildings? When you think about it, the answer must be no.

What would people think if someone said they were going to completely build over this untouched area of wetland:

Venetian lagoon, Venice, Italy

Most people would probably think it was quite a terrible idea. But actually this is exactly the sort of place where Venice was built — and a lot of people think Venice is one of the most beautiful cities in the world and they're very glad indeed that it was built.

The fields and ponds were turned into this:

If we are being really honest, what we dislike so much is not buildings: it is ugly buildings. The problem is not that there are too many cities, but that there are too many ugly cities.

The shocking thing is that we have given up imagining that we could build wonderful, delightful and enchanting cities. If someone says, 'Let's build a new city!' we will automatically imagine something horrible — and that's strange, because we know that in the past it was completely possible to build delightful cities. We just assume that we can't do the same. So we protect the land and as a consequence houses and flats become hugely expensive.

We've got more money than ever before, we build more than ever before and we've got much, much better technology than we had in the past, but the fact is that people long ago built the cities we love and we build cities we dislike. They built Paris and Edinburgh and Bath and Venice and lots of other charming places and we don't build anything nearly as lovely.

The problem is our ideas.

In this book, we've been trying to find good ideas for making attractive buildings, so that in the future we can make cities that are as lovely — or even more lovely — than the best cities of the past. And if we did that, nice houses and flats wouldn't be nearly so expensive.

Architecture and democracy

The big idea we want to end with is *democracy*. Democracy means asking everyone what they think and then doing the thing that most people prefer. Imagine you were planning a class trip and there are two suggestions: Visit a farm or visit a castle. Where should the class go? The democratic solution would be to take a vote. If only four or so people want to go to the farm and fifteen people want to go to the castle, then you go to the castle.

Most architects believe in democracy when it comes down to choosing a political leader — but they don't believe in it when it comes to choosing a good building. We think they might be wrong in this...

We think the idea of democracy could help us to build much nicer cities.

Suppose there was a vote about buildings and places. You could ask the general public to vote on all sorts of homes, buildings, public spaces and even whole towns and cities!

Take a look at the pictures on the next two pages and see if you can work out which ones you prefer and why.

Which buildings do you find more beautiful?

What about these streets?

Rue de Meaux Housing Complex, Paris, France, 1991

Ainslie Place, Edinburgh, Scotland, 1822–1858

In both these cases, we think most people would probably prefer the second example.

If we used democracy to inform architecture we would likely build a lot more nice streets and buildings because these are the sorts of places that most people want to live in. It would make a lot of sense to be democratic about buildings because everyone has to see them all the time. But this is not what happens at the moment. Architecture affects everyone but we have generally left the big decisions about how cities look to *just a few people*: we leave it to professional architects.

That's a big problem. Architects are usually very lovely people, of course. But they don't necessarily think about buildings in the same way that everyone else does.

If you asked architects what kind of buildings they'd like to build, many of them would go for the first example. Architects often like the sorts of buildings that other people don't. (The buildings in the first examples were designed by architects who won big prizes for their works — prizes given by other architects.) Why do you think this happens?

Generally, people don't learn about architecture at school, and only a few people study it at university, so only people who are particularly interested in buildings ever think of architecture as a career. They then spend years and years talking to other architects about buildings.

Architects want to build things that excite *other architects*.

This building is in Sydney, Australia. It kind of looks like it is falling down or maybe it's melting. It was designed by one of the most well-known architects in the world, Frank Gehry.

Dr Chau Chak Wing Building, University of Technology, Sydney, Australia, 2012–2014

Other architects find it interesting because it is a really complicated design. They get bored of making attractive, simple buildings so they want to make things that look unusual and strange.

But the real goal should be:

Make buildings and cities that most people like and to make lots and lots of them.

If we had a vote about the kinds of buildings people actually liked, cities would look a lot nicer and be really wonderful places to live and work.

We wrote this book to help you think about architecture; but it's not just about thinking, maybe one day you can put some of these ideas into action and help us to build a more beautiful world. We hope you will!

Manarola, Cinque Terre, Italy

Image References

p. 1	Michael L. Baird / Flickr
p. 2	Cultura Creative (RF) / Alamy Stock Photo
p. 3t	Stephen Dorey / Alamy Stock Photo
p. 3b	Image provided by Hannes Coudenys / The Architectural Review
p. 4	fokke baarssen / Shutterstock
p. 5	Anastase Maragos / Unsplash
p. 6	Gugerell / Wikimedia Commons
p. 7	ajay_suresh / Flickr (CC BY 2.0)
p. 8	Sorasak / Unsplash
p. 11	Miranda Ash2006 / Flickr (CC BY-NC 2.0)
p. 12	Nils Versemann / Dreamstime
p. 13	mTaira / Shutterstock
p. 14	BSTAR IMAGES / Alamy Stock Photo
p. 15	Rainer Ebert / Wikimedia Commons
p. 16t	Bildarchiv Monheim GmbH / Alamy Stock Photo
p. 16b	Paul Sableman / Flickr (CC BY 2.0)
p. 17	David Iliff (Diliff) / Wikimedia Commons (CC BY-SA 3.0)
p. 18	Carol M. Highsmith Archive, Library of Congress
p. 19	Allen McGregor / Flickr (CC BY 2.0)
p. 20	Vinogradova Alyona / Shutterstock
p. 21	allOver images / Alamy Stock Photo
p. 22	Photo © Neil Poole (neil mp) / Flickr
p. 25	Fran Jacquier / Unsplash
p. 27	Kinshuk Bose / Unsplash
p. 29t	Danichou / Wikimedia Commons
p. 29b	Jebulon / Wikimedia Commons
p. 30	Alexander Mooi / Flickr (CC BY 2.0)
p. 31	Gandolfo Cannatella / 123rf
p. 32	Nono vlf / Wikimedia Commons (CC BY-SA 4.0)
p. 33	terren in Virginia / Flickr (CC BY 2.0)
p. 34	Livioandronico2013 / Wikimedia Commons (CC BY-SA 4.0)
p. 35	Glen Bowman / Wikimedia Commons (CC BY-SA 2.0)
p. 36	Andrea Palladio, The Four Books of Architecture, 1570. Internet Archive Book Images / Flickr
p. 37	robertharding / Alamy Stock Photo
p. 38	David Lyons / Alamy Stock Photo
p. 39	Brian McNeil / Wikimedia Commons (CC BY 3.0)
p. 40	Philip Larson / Flickr (CC BY-SA 2.0)
p. 41	Yann Forget / Wikimedia Commons (CC-BY-SA)
p. 42	John Fielding / Flickr (CC BY 2.0)
p. 43	Moonik / Wikimedia Commons (CC BY-SA 3.0)
p. 44	Image provided by ONBob and TOBuilt (ACO Toronto)
p. 45	Oleknutlee / Wikipedia
p. 46t	Robert Stainforth / Alamy Stock Photo
p. 46b	Martin Bond / Alamy Stock Photo
p. 47	Colin Underhill / Alamy Stock Photo
p. 48	AlexZaitsev / Shutterstock
p. 49	Darryl Brooks / Shutterstock
p. 50	Ice Tea / Unsplash
p. 51	Robin Benzrihem / Unsplash
p. 52t	Desintegrator / Alamy Stock Photo
p. 52b	Bob Linsdell / Wikimedia Commons (CC BY 3.0)
p. 53	Alexander Spatari / Getty Images
p. 54	Sara Groblechner / Unsplash
p. 55	dpa picture alliance / Alamy Stock Photo
p. 56	Ma Fushun / Unsplash
p. 57	Ingus Kruklitis / Shutterstock
p. 58t	Image provided by Vinesh Pomal
p. 58b	ACME / Flickr (CC BY-NC 2.0)
p. 61	Peter Cook-VIEW / Alamy Stock Photo
p. 67	Grzegorz Kordus / Dreamstime
p. 68t	.Martin. / Flickr (CC BY-ND 2.0)
p. 68b	Mr Stan Zemanek / Wikimedia Commons (CC BY-SA 3.0)
p. 69	David Kleyn / Alamy Stock Photo
p. 70t	VenusInTaurus / Flickr (CC BY-NC 2.0)
p. 70b	Photo © Cynthia Meyer
p. 71	FLHC A29 / Alamy Stock Photo
p. 72	Harold / Wikimedia Commons (CC BY-SA 3.0)
p. 73	Julian Castle / Alamy Stock Photo
p. 74	Fred Bigio / Flickr (CC BY 2.0)
p. 75	Richard Cooke / Alamy Stock Photo
p. 76	Alex Atudosie / Unsplash
p. 77	The World Of Sports Sc / Shutterstock
p. 79	Serhii Chrucky / Alamy Stock Photo
p. 80	Martell Brighten / Shutterstock
p. 82	Josh Hallett / Wikimedia Commons (CC BY-SA 2.0)
p. 83	Rodrigo Kugnharski / Unsplash
p. 84	Thomon / Wikimedia Commons (CC BY-SA 4.0)
p. 85	Jean Béraud, Paris Kiosk, c. 1880–1884 Oil on canvas, 35.5 cm x 26.5 cm. Walters Art Museum, Baltimore, Maryland, USA Acquired by Henry Walters, 1901. / Wikimedia Commons
p. 86	JOHN TOWNER / Unsplash
p. 87	Pierre Petit, Baron Georges-Eugène Haussmann (1809–1891), 1860. Bibliothèque nationale de France, Paris / Wikimedia Commons
p. 88	Cinematographer / Shutterstock
p. 89	Jon Arnold Images Ltd / Alamy Stock Photo
p. 90	Sarbescu Radu / Shutterstock
p. 91	Mattinbgn / Wikimedia Commons (CC BY 3.0)
p. 92	Marco Mariani / Shutterstock
p. 93	Panther Media GmbH / Alamy Stock Photo
p. 94	Savvapanf Photo / Shutterstock
p. 95	Hans Hillewaert / Wikimedia Commons (CC BY-SA 3.0)
p. 96	Andrea Cau / Unsplash
p. 97	NASA / Flickr